T0278504

EVOLUTION & CULTURAL INFLUENCES OF MUSIC

ROCK

EVOLUTION & CULTURAL INFLUENCES OF MUSIC

COUNTRY
ELECTRONIC DANCE MUSIC (EDM)
HIP-HOP
LATIN AND CARIBBEAN
POP MUSIC
R&B, SOUL, AND GOSPEL
ROCK
STAGE AND SCREEN

EVOLUTION & CULTURAL INFLUENCES OF MUSIC

ROCK

JAMES JORDAN

MASON CREST

PHILADELPHIA | MIAMI

MASON CREST
450 Parkway Drive, Suite D, Broomall, Pennsylvania 19008
(866) MCP-BOOK (toll-free) • www.masoncrest.com

Printed and bound in the United States of America.

CPSIA Compliance Information: Batch #ECIM2019.
For further information, contact Mason Crest at 1-866-MCP-Book.

First printing

ISBN (hardback) 978-1-4222-4376-3
ISBN (series) 978-1-4222-4369-5
ISBN (ebook) 978-1-4222-7441-5

Library of Congress Cataloging-in-Publication Data on file at the Library of Congress.

Interior and cover design: Torque Advertising + Design
Production: Michelle Luke

QR CODES AND LINKS TO THIRD-PARTY CONTENT

CONTENTS

KEY ICONS TO LOOK FOR:

 Words to Understand: These words with their easy-to-understand definitions will increase the reader's understanding of the text while building vocabulary skills.

 Sidebars: This boxed material within the main text allows readers to build knowledge, gain insights, explore possibilities, and broaden their perspectives by weaving together additional information to provide realistic and holistic perspectives.

 Educational Videos: Readers can view videos by scanning our QR codes, providing them with additional educational content to supplement the text. Examples include news coverage, moments in history, speeches, iconic sports moments, and much more!

 Text-Dependent Questions: These questions send the reader back to the text for more careful attention to the evidence presented there.

 Research Projects: Readers are pointed toward areas of further inquiry connected to each chapter. Suggestions are provided for projects that encourage deeper research and analysis.

 Series Glossary of Key Terms: This back-of-the-book glossary contains terminology used throughout this series. Words found here increase the reader's ability to read and comprehend higher-level books and articles in this field.

Statue of Elvis Presley in downtown Memphis, Tennessee. The "king of Rock and Roll" became an American cultural icon in the 1950s thanks to hits like "Don't Be Cruel," "Hound Dog," and "Heartbreak Hotel."

 # WORDS TO UNDERSTAND

LP record—a vinyl disc containing about twenty-two minutes of music on each side, which was played on a record player at 33 revolutions per minute (rpm).

rhythm and blues—a style of music played primarily by black people, that evolved into rock and roll music with some other infuences.

segregation—the practice of keeping one group or race separated from another.

single—a record that is released by a musician and intended to be played on the radio. Singles generally have an A side, containing the song that's expected to be a hit, and a B side, containing another song. Singles were also called "45s," because they were released on smaller seven-inch record disks that were played at 45 rpm.

transistor—a device that regulates the flow of electricity and acts as a switch or gate for electronic signals.

CHAPTER 1

Origins of Rock and Roll

Rock and roll music originated in the late 1940s and early 1950s, but pinning down a specific place, time, or person who started rock is impossible. It developed in several places at the same time, and drew influences from many different musical genres, including jazz, **rhythm and blues** (R&B), country and western, and gospel music. Rock and roll took American society by storm in the 1950s, and soon became the most popular music style in the country.

Over the decades rock music has changed and branched out in many directions, yet the basic elements of the music remain the same. Rock songs are often played at a fast tempo. Many songs often follow a musical pattern of twelve measures, with four beats in each measure. A common three-chord pattern is known as the "twelve-bar blues." Songs are usually played on amplified instruments, such as electric guitars.

Usually, rock music is played by small groups of three to six musicians. A typical rock band might have two electric guitar players, a bass guitarist, and a drummer. The lead guitarist plays the song's melody, and often performs an instrumental solo. The rhythm guitarist accompanies him by playing chords that compliment the melody. The bass guitarist and the drummer establish the beat and rhythm of the song. In some bands musicians playing keyboards, horns, or other instruments may be added to create a fuller sound. A vocalist will sing the lyrics energetically, sometimes screaming or shouting to be heard above the band.

Origins of a Genre

It is impossible to talk about the history of rock and roll without understanding what the United States was like at the end of World War II in the mid-1940s. In many parts of the country, white and black Americans did not mix. Blacks faced racial discrimination in their everyday lives. They were not allowed to live in the same neighborhoods as whites. Schools, restaurants, and other public places were **segregated**.

Entertainment was also segregated. Theaters and nightclubs either were not open to blacks, or had a small section in the back where they could sit. The music of black and white artists

The development of the electric guitar made rock music possible. Electric guitars use devices called pickups to convert the vibration of the strings into an electrical signal, which can be played back loudly through an amplifier.

were recorded and sold by different companies. Even radio stations were segregated, and most radio stations would usually only play records by white artists.

Music could also be a barrier-breaker, however. During the 1920s, white audiences had begun to enjoy musical styles that originated in black communities, such as jazz or blues. Jazz music came from the South, particularly New Orleans. It was fun, upbeat music that made people want to dance. The melodies were played on trumpets and other brass instruments, and talented musicians often improvised wild solos. Rhythm and blues music also originated in the South, in places like Mississippi and Tennessee. Blues songs usually had a strong rhythm and simple three-chord structure. The lyrics often expressed pain, sadness, and suffering.

Scan here to learn more about the origins of rock and roll music:

Segregation was common in the United States during the 1940s and 1950s. This segregated movie theater for black Americans was located in Leland, Mississippi.

Over time, the bands that played jazz and blues began adding more musicians and different instruments. During the 1930s and 1940s, white bandleaders incorporated jazz and blues rhythms and sounds into their own music. Sometimes, they hired black musicians to play with their bands. And black bandleaders like Duke Ellington and Count Basie were just as popular with white audiences as with black audiences.

Several technological developments in the late 1940s made rock and roll music possible. One was the development of the electric guitar, thanks to innovators like Les Paul and Leon Fender.

Before this time guitars had been used to accompany the music; now they could provide a dominant sound. Another innovation was the creation of the "long play" record format; more songs could be included on the new **LP records**. A third development was the invention of the **transistor** in 1947, which made it possible to make small handheld radios in the early 1950s. For the first time, music could be portable, and put into the hands of young people.

Black Music for White Audiences

Due to the racial attitudes of the time, parents tended to frown on their teenagers bringing home records by black musicians. But the music was very popular among young people. Record companies began looking for white singers who could perform the songs. White musicians took ideas freely from black musicians, and they often played together.

Early rock and roll stars like Fats Domino believed that the musical form was just a new way to market the music black artists like him had been playing for a long time. "Rock & roll is nothing but rhythm & blues and we've been playing it for years down in New Orleans," he once said. The early rock and roll stars acknowledged the influence of black musicians.

Unfortunately, black musicians often did not benefit as much financially as the white musicians did. Sometimes, music companies would purchased the rights to play a song from the original writer for a flat fee. If the record sold a lot of copies, the profit would all go to the music company, not the original writer. Publishing royalties were not common at the time. Still, if a famous white singer's re-recording of a black performer's song sold a million copies, the original recording would sell more copies too. That helped some black musicians, although indirectly.

White musicians also made important contributions to rock and roll. Traditional country music—sometimes called

FEMALE ROCKER ROSETTA THARP

Gospel music star Sister Rosetta Tharp (1915–1973) was also a rock and roll pioneer. Some say her 1944 song "Strange Things Happening" was the first rock and roll song. Not just a singer, she also played the electric guitar. This was extremely unusual for a woman, yet she is said to have been better than any male guitarist as well. "Nobody—not Chuck Berry, not Scotty Moore [Elvis Presley's famed guitarist], not James Burton, not Keith Richards—played wilder or more primal rock 'n' roll guitar than [Tharp]," claimed a article in *The Guardian*. "With a Gibson SG in her hands, Sister Rosetta could raise the dead. And that was before she started to sing."

Tharp was also unconventional because she was not afraid to play her gospel music in regular nightclubs, which many Christians frowned upon. She became the first gospel performer to have a number one hit on the R&B music chart. She gave a concert in England in 1964 that had a major impact on the evolution of rock and roll in that country. Many great rock stars—including Johnny Cash, Elvis Presley, Little Richard, and Bob Dylan—said she was a major influence on their music. She was inducted into the Rock and Roll Hall of Fame in 2018 for her early contributions to the genre.

"hillbilly music" because it originated in the rural Appalachian Mountain region—was an important influence. In the 1940s and early 1950s, Hank Williams became famous for singing "brutally honest songs about his life in the language of the everyman," according to the Rock and Roll Hall of Fame. Some white performers took these country songs and played them at a faster

Until the late 1940s, each side of a record could hold only about four minutes of music. The "long play" (LP) album format, introduced in 1948, could hold more than twenty minutes of music per side. This changed the way popular music was marketed, as artists could include ten to twelve short songs on each LP album.

R&B tempo so that they would be better for dancing. This early form of rock music was known as "rockabilly."

Cultural historian Gregory McNamee has written on the blending of black and white musical styles to create rock music. "A mixture of white and black musical forms from the Mississippi Delta, country music with the grinding of machinery and automobiles implicit in its grinding beat, rhythm and blues spread across the nation from its birthplace, Detroit," he wrote in an essay on the origins of the genre. "When white pop music

"Rock Around the Clock," recorded by Bill Haley and the Comets, became a big hit in 1955. Although it was not the first rock and roll song, it is credited with bringing the new music into the mainstream of American youth culture.

entered the idiom in the immediate postwar era, rhythm and blues became rock and roll."

The First Rock and Roll Song

Some rock and roll historians credit the song "Rocket 88," released in 1951, as the first rock and roll record. The song was written by Ike Turner, and sung by Jackie Brenston. It sounds similar to later rock and roll music, with a distorted guitar sound and rock-like rhythm. Rock and roll pioneer Sam Phillips, who would later discover Elvis Presley and other stars, recorded "Rocket 88" in his studio.

Another candidate is Roy Brown, who released "Good Rocking Tonight" in 1947, and "Rocking at Midnight" in 1948. He was one of the first to use the term "rock" in this fashion. A more upbeat remake of "Good Rocking Tonight," released by Wynonie Harris in 1948, is also sometimes called the first rock and roll song.

Most agree, however, that the first important rock and roll hit was "Rock Around the Clock," a song written in 1952 by two black artists, Max Freedman and James Myers. It was recorded in 1954 by a white performer, Bill Haley, and his band the Comets. "Even though you'll find things with an even earlier recording date that sound just like rock and roll, you have to say that 'Rock Around the Clock' was the first record that really brought everything together, that made tremors around the world," says music editor Tony Cajiao.

Interestingly enough, Bill Haley did not believe "Rock Around the Clock" was going to be a hit at first. At the time, musicians released their hit songs on small seven-inch records called **singles**, which included a song on each side. The "A side" would include the best song, the one that was supposed to be played on the radio. On the other side of the record, called the "B side," was usually a song that was not considered a prospective hit. Bill Haley and the Comets had released a single with a song called "Thirteen Women" on the A side. It was a modest hit. The B side, "Rock Around the Clock," did not get noticed until it was used in a movie released in 1955. But it soon became a huge hit, and put rock music on the map.

The "Birthplace" of Rock and Roll

Because all sorts of musical influences came together to create the rock and roll genre, several places claim to be the "birthplace" of rock and roll. Memphis, Tennessee, is one city

The Rock and Roll Hall of Fame and Museum is located in Cleveland, Ohio. It includes displays commemorating the history of rock music and the genre's most influential performers.

that makes this claim. In the early twentieth century Memphis was home to one of the original blues composers, W.C. Handy. In the early 1950s Memphis was the location of Sun Records, a company owned by Sam Phillips. During the 1950s Phillips recorded "Rocket 88" and other songs black R&B artists like B.B. King and Chester "Howlin' Wolf" Burnett, as well as early white rock performers like Elvis Presley, Carl Perkins, Jerry Lee Lewis, Johnny Cash, and Roy Orbison. Another important music company in Memphis was Stax Records, which gave a start to R&B artists like Otis Redding, Sam and Dave, and Booker T and the MG's.

A Cleveland, Ohio, disc jockey named Alan Freed is said to be the first person who used the term "rock and roll" to describe the new style of music. In 1951 Freed was hired at radio station WJW to play classical music, but he recognized that young people liked R&B music more. He talked the radio station manager into letting him play records by black R&B performers for an hour each week. In 1952, Freed also organized what some call the first rock concert in 1952. He later moved to a radio station in New York, where he would help rock and roll reach an even larger audience.

Hattiesburg, Mississippi, has a claim because of its roots in gospel music. In 1936, gospel singers Roosevelt and Uaroy Graves recorded two non-religious songs that became hits, "Barbeque Bust," and "Dangerous Woman." Author Robert Palmer, a scholar of the blues, once noted that "The Graves brothers' 'Barbecue Bust' and 'Dangerous Woman' featured fully formed rock and roll guitar riffs and a stomping rock and roll beat."

Detroit, Michigan, doesn't have as strong of a claim as the birthplace of rock and roll, but it was an important center for rhythm and blues music in the 1940s. In the 1960s, Detroit would also be the starting point for the Motown sound in the 1960s, and later for punk rock music—both significant developments in rock and roll history.

Rock and roll marked a blending of many styles of music from people of very diverse backgrounds. That is why it is hard to define exactly when it started and where it came from. The music changed our culture as technology made those changes possible. It is no surprise that rock and roll has since evolved into the many different styles of rock music that exist today.

TEXT-DEPENDENT QUESTIONS

1. What technological breakthroughs in the late 1940s contributed to rock and roll?
2. What are some musical genres that were blended into rock and roll?
3. Why was Memphis, Tennessee, important in the early days of rock and roll?

RESEARCH PROJECT

Look up some material on the history of rock and roll. Some say rock music was just rhythm and blues repackaged for a white audience. Do some research on how it developed and write a paper describing how you feel about that question.

Black musicians like Chuck Berry, Bo Diddley, Fats Domino, and Little Richard (pictured performing here) had a huge influence on the creation of rock and roll music in the 1950s. They were among the genre's first major stars.

 WORDS TO UNDERSTAND

blackball—to prevent someone from working in a particular field or industry.

cover—to perform a song someone else has written and previously performed.

payola—the practice by small record labels of making secret cash payments to disc jockeys so that they would play their records on the air.

social upheaval—a sudden change to the political or social norms of a country or community.

CHAPTER 2

The Rockin' 1950s

By the mid-1950s, the stage was set for the musical explosion that became rock and roll. Young people—particularly those born after the end of World War II in 1945—would fuel this explosion. In previous generations, most young people would go to work once they reached the age of fourteen or so. After the war, there was an economic boom, and American families had jobs and money. There were more opportunities for teenagers to pursue recreational activities and entertainment. Without teenagers, there would have been no market for rock and roll music.

New technologies were emerging that made the spread of music much easier. Styles were also being blended, with "black" rhythm and blues mixing with "white" country and popular music, as well as jazz, folk and other styles. The combination of musical elements appealed to the new generation. If their parents did not like the new music, that was even better.

"It was so much more vital and alive than any music we had ever heard before that it needed a new category," wrote Robert Palmer, a journalist and music critic, in an essay in *Rolling Stone* magazine. "Rock and roll was much more than new music for us. It was an obsession, and a way of life. Because it was obviously, inarguably our music."

Social Statement

The 1950s were also a time of **social upheaval** in the United States. In 1954, the US Supreme Court ruled that segregated "separate but equal" schools were unconstitutional. This ruling was soon expanded to eliminate segregation in transportation and public facilities. In 1955, Rosa Parks refused to sit in the back of a bus in Montgomery, Alabama. Her arrest drew national attention, and sparked the civil rights movement led by Martin Luther King Jr. and others.

Music was another area where the barriers that separated black and white Americans were crumbling. By the 1950s, white artists were **covering** songs written or originally performed by black artists. Some white radio stations began to play music by both black and white artists. Rock and roll would help to erase the line between "black" music and "white" music—at least in the minds of many young people.

Scan here to learn more about Rosa Parks and the civil rights movement:

Some people claim Sun Studio in Memphis, Tennessee, is the birthplace of rock 'n' roll music. During the 1950s most of the biggest stars of rock music, including Elvis Presley, Carl Perkins, Jerry Lee Lewis, Johnny Cash, and Roy Orbison, recorded there. Today it is a National Historic Landmark.

Independent Record Studios

The emergence of the small independent recording studio was also key to the development of rock and roll. Large record companies preferred to focus on making music that would not offend anyone. They continued to record the big bands and vocal groups that had been popular during the war years. It was the small independent studios that pushed the boundaries and brought rock and roll into the public arena.

People like Sam Phillips were visionary pioneers in the music industry of the 1950s. Thanks to new recording technologies, they were able to produce professional-sounding records just like the major labels. Phillips owned Sun Records in Memphis, which was typical of the very small operations. It was a one-man operation at first. People could come in off the street, and record whatever they wanted, and Phillips would put it onto a record for them.

Sam Phillips had grown up in rural Alabama, where many of his neighbors were black Americans who farmed cotton. He heard and appreciated their music. As a young man during the 1940s, he had worked as a disk jockey for a radio station in Alabama that played both white and black music. Phillips saw the potential for blending of the music. When he started Sun Records, he had a vision for what popular music could be. He set out to develop talent and give musicians a platform. "Everyone knew that I was just a struggling cat down here trying to develop new and different artists, and get some freedom in music, and tap some resources and people that weren't being tapped," he later said.

Legend has it that Elvis Presley walked into Sun Records one day in 1953 to make a recording for his mother. His singing talent was noticed, and the next year Phillips began recording and promoting Elvis. In 1955 Elvis's song "That's All Right Mama," became a regional hit. It was a cover of a song written and originally performed by a black artist, Arthur "Big Boy" Crudup. Later that year, Phillips had some financial trouble, so he sold Presley's contract to RCA, a major label. He lost Elvis, but received enough money to promote other artists, such as Carl Perkins, whose "Blue Suede Shoes" became Sun Records's first national hit. He also recorded Jerry Lee Lewis, Johnny Cash, and Roy Orbison.

Songwriter and guitarist Chuck Berry inspired some of rock music's most important songwriters, including John Lennon and Paul McCartney of the Beatles and Keith Richards and Mick Jagger of the Rolling Stones.

Sun Records was far from the only small independent label that succeeded with rock and roll music. Chess Records in Chicago released recordings by blues performers like Chester "Howlin' Wolf" Burnett, Chuck Berry, and Bo Diddley. Imperial Records recorded both Fats Domino and Ricky Nelson, a white singer whose song "Poor Little Fool" became the first #1 hit on *Billboard* magazine's new Hot 100 chart in 1958. And Stax Records, Specialty Records, and Atlantic were among the other small labels making hit rock and roll records.

Elvis Becomes a Star

Elvis would become rock and roll's biggest star of the 1950s. RCA was one of the country's largest music labels, and owned television and radio stations. It could promote and market music across the nation. In 1956, Elvis's single "Heartbreak Hotel" became the top-selling record in the country. It was the first of Presley's six hits that year, followed by "I Want You, I Need You, I Love You," "Hound Dog," "Don't Be Cruel," and "Love Me Tender," all of which hit #1 on the *Billboard* chart, and a cover of "Blue Suede Shoes," which reached #24.

On September 9, 1956, Elvis appeared on the *Ed Sullivan Show*, one of the most popular television programs of the time. Elvis performed four songs and created a national scandal when he swiveled his hips suggestively. Many adults, particularly the entertainment critics, didn't know what to make of it all. But Ed Sullivan and his producers recognized talent when they saw it, and Elvis was invited back two more times. (In later appearances, Sullivan told the cameraman to shoot Elvis from the waist up!)

Elvis would become one of the most famous entertainers in the world. He would record thirty #1 hits during his long career, and would appear in many popular movies. Due to his impact, rock-and-roll fans still remember Elvis fondly as "the King."

ROCK AND ROLL ON TV

Television was very important to the popularity of rock and roll. In the 1950s, the medium was just coming into its own as the premier mode of entertainment in America. The *Ed Sullivan Show* was a popular program that sometimes aired rock performers, including Elvis in 1956 and the Beatles in 1964. But many local TV stations produced their own shows specifically for rock and roll. One such show was *Bandstand*, which premiered in 1952 on TV station WFIL in Philadelphia. On August 5, 1957, the show was renamed *American Bandstand* and broadcast on sixty-seven stations coast to coast. The host was Dick Clark, who for ninety minutes each afternoon featured top American rock 'n' roll acts as well as a studio dance floor filled with teenagers gyrating on camera to the music. Within a year of its debut, 40 million kids a day hurried home after school to turn on *American Bandstand*.

Texas musician Buddy Holly was one of the biggest rock and roll stars of the 1950s. With his band the Crickets, he recorded such hits as "That'll Be the Day," "Peggy Sue," and "Everyday." At the height of his fame, while touring the Midwest with other rock and roll stars, he was killed in an airplane crash.

Black Rock and Roll Stars

The popularity of Elvis, Bill Haley, and other white rock and roll stars—whose songs drew on African-American influences—helped pave the way for black artists to achieve mainstream success in rock and roll. One of these black artists was Chuck Berry. He mixed the sounds of country guitar and rhythm and blues. He sang about subjects that teenagers liked, such as cars, girls, and school. Berry scored hits with songs such as "Maybellene," "Johnny B. Goode," and "No Particular Place to Go." He would greatly influence many later rockers.

Little Richard, born Richard Wayne Penniman in 1932, was another influential African-American rock and roll star. Hits such as "Tutti Frutti" "Long Tall Sally," and "Good Golly Miss Molly"—along with a manic stage presence—made him popular with young people of all backgrounds. At a time when segregation was still common in the South, black and white fans mixed freely at Little Richard's concerts.

As a teenager, Bo Diddley learned to play the violin and trombone. But, dazzled by the artistry of bluesmen like John Lee Hooker and Muddy Waters, he took up the guitar. Playing his trademark rectangular guitar, Diddley delighted fans with such favorites as "Who Do You Love?" and "I'm a Man." His songs were widely covered.

The Coasters were among the first African-American groups to sing rock 'n' roll. They burst onto the scene with 1957's "Young Blood." Other hits included "Yakety Yak" and "Charlie Brown," which both were humorous songs.

Piano player Antoine "Fats" Domino got his start in boogie-woogie music. In 1955, Imperial Records released his first album, *Carry on Rockin'*. Over the next ten years, he scored many rock and pop hits, including "'Aint that a Shame" and "Blueberry Hill."

The Power of the DJ

While there were a lot of record companies making records, it was the radio disc jockeys of the 1950s who controlled what music was played. They were the gatekeepers, in a sense, because the songs they decided to play were the ones that people heard on the radio. Listeners might decide to buy a single of a popular song, or an LP album that included the song. Consequently, DJs had a lot of control over what became popular.

One of the most famous DJs of the 1950s was Alan Freed. The DJ from Cleveland, Ohio, was independent and played songs by both black and white artists. He was also the first to call the new music "Rock and Roll."

Not all DJs were white. Douglas "Jocko" Henderson was a black American who worked as a DJ in Baltimore, Philadelphia, and New York City. "The 'Ace from Outer Space,' a pioneering African-American DJ, was known for his rhythmic patter and buttery baritone," noted a CNN profile.

Because of the power of popular DJs, some record labels paid them secretly so that they would play the new records by their artists. This practice became known as **payola**. Some DJs received tens of thousands of dollars from record companies.

In 1959, the US Congress began investigating the practice of payola. There had previously been Congressional hearing over television game shows where the outcome was "fixed," or determined in advance. To many people, payola was simply bribery. Although DJs protested that the payments did not influence what they played on the air, the system seemed corrupt.

Freed denied having accepted payola, but he lost his job and was **blackballed** from the music industry. Dick Clark also denied taking payments. Clark had owned stock in some record companies, but sold them when the investigations began. He managed to save his career.

Alan Freed is credited with naming the emerging music of the 1950s "rock and roll," but the payola scandal of the late 1950s cost Freed his career as a DJ.

This photo of Elvis Presley was taken to promote the 1957 film Jailhouse Rock. *Elvis would make more than thirty films during the 1950s and 1960s, often recording hit songs to accompany them.*

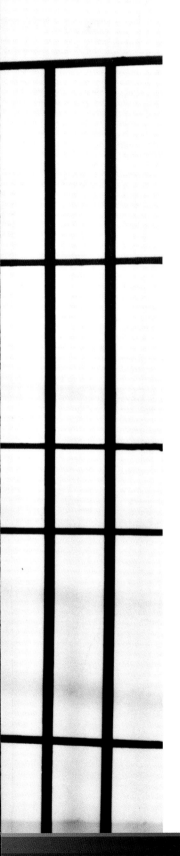

The payola scandal was a major blow to disc jockeys and radio stations. Radio station directors began controlling what DJs could play during their shows, taking away most of their power. The scandal also contributed to the demise of the independent recording label. Without payola to even the playing field, it became much harder for the independent studio to get its songs played. The major labels, which had once ignored rock and roll, now gradually took over recording and selling the music.

Looking Ahead

The 1950s were a wild ride for rock and roll. Performers led the way in determining what was "cool"—not only in music but in clothing, hairstyle, and even politics. By the end of the decade, rock and roll was firmly entrenched in American life, and was developing an international following. "Fifties rock and roll ... proved more than a passing fad or an episode of youthful folly," writes Robert Palmer. "It has provided the model, the template, the jumping-off point for virtually every subsequent wave of pop-music innovation.

However, the industry had suffered through the payola scandal. Some of rock's biggest stars were also facing challenges. Elvis was drafted into the US Army, and served a two-year term. Chuck Berry was busted for drugs and sent to jail.

Little Richard quit to preach the gospel. Jerry Lee Lewis was blackballed from the industry after causing a scandal by marrying his very young second cousin. And in February 1959, three of rock's biggest stars, Buddy Holly, Richie Valens, and JP "Big Bopper" Richardson died in a plane crash in Iowa. Some people saw this as "the day the music died."

The 1960s would see a new infusion of energy that would vitalize and change rock music, and the genre would continue to evolve and grow.

TEXT-DEPENDENT QUESTIONS

1. Who was Sam Phillips?
2. Why did the payola scandal occur?
3. What was "the day the music died?"

RESEARCH PROJECT

In your school library, or with the Internet, look up some articles about the very early days of rock and roll. White musicians "covered" songs that had been released by black musicians. While the black musicians were paid, they received no royalties. Write about about your feelings on this issue. Is it just to pay someone for a song and not give them royalties?

The Beatles were at the forefront of a wave of British rock groups that became popular in the United States. Crowds of screaming girls greeted the Beatles at every public appearance, and young men copied their "mop-top" hairdos. The group included rhythm guitarist John Lennon, drummer Ringo Starr, bass guitarist Paul McCartney, and lead guitarist George Harrison.

 WORDS TO UNDERSTAND

music festival—a gathering where multiple rock bands perform, usually over two or three days.

pop culture—activities, practices, or commercial products that most people enjoy or appreciate.

prolific songwriter—someone who produces or composes a lot of songs.

tour—a series of concerts that an artist performs over a period of time to promote their music.

CHAPTER 3

Rock and Roll Evolves

If the 1950s were the birth and infancy of rock and roll, the 1960s became the art form's teen years. By this time, rock and roll had moved far beyond the borders of the United States. Though it originated in America, it was developing in England, Germany, and other European countries.

One way that rock and roll spread was through young musicians listening to hit records, and playing what they had heard. In his autobiography, Bob Dylan said that he and his friends used to drive more than a hundred miles just to listen to a folk music album they had heard that someone possessed. When they "listened," they actually spent hours with the record, playing it over and over and trying to mimic the sound with their guitars and other instruments.

Young musicians also learned by watching other musicians. As rock and roll music became popular, both black and white artists went on **tour** in Great Britain and Europe during the late 1950s. These tours gave European musicians a chance to see the performers, and copy their music. A 1960 tour of England by guitarist Rosetta Tharpe was particularly influential. Keith Richards, who would become famous as the guitarist for the Rolling Stones, said that her style affected the way he played guitar.

The music world changed significantly during the period in the mid-1960s, thanks to the emergence of the Beatles, Bob Dylan, and the Motown Sound. There were many other influences on rock music, but these three had arguably the greatest impact on the genre.

Surf Music and Protest Songs

In the early 1960s, rock and roll stars like Elvis and Roy Orbison were still releasing hit records. But distinctive new sounds were beginning to appear as well. The Beach Boys were among the first groups to popularize the California surf sound. They sang harmonic, light-hearted songs about the joys of beach days, surfing, chasing girls, and racing cars. In 1963, the group Surfaris recorded "Wipe Out," an instrumental hit that showed just how dominant the electric guitar had become in rock 'n' roll music.

On the acoustic side, there was also a strong folk music scene developing that would have its own impact on rock and roll. Folk artists like Joan Baez, Pete Seeger, and the trio Peter, Paul, and Mary recorded hit songs in the early 1960s. Folk songs often focused on lyrics about politics and current events, tying them into the youth culture. However, many young people were rock music fans, not folk music fans.

Robert Zimmerman—better known as Bob Dylan—was one of the major players of the folk music revival. Dylan had been heavily influenced by Woody Guthrie, a folk musician who had written protest songs during the 1930s. Dylan continued that tradition, but put his own mark on the music as well.

As a young man Dylan moved to New York City, where he quickly became part of the folk music scene. He played in a lot of clubs and eventually was signed to a major label as a recording artist. He had a nasal-toned, raspy voice and his guitar playing was average at best. Still, his words had poetic meaning and touched people in a deep way.

For his many contributions to American music and society, Bob Dylan received the Presidential Medal of Freedom—the nation's highest civilian honor—from President Barack Obama in 2012.

He was a **prolific songwriter**, and during the 1960s his songs spoke to young people who were concerned about the tumultuous changes in American society. "Blowing in the Wind," and "Hard Rain's a-Gonna Fall," were released in 1963. That year the civil rights movement was reaching its peak, with Martin Luther King Jr. giving his "I Have a Dream" speech in Washington, D.C., in August. Later that year came the shocking assassination of President John F. Kennedy, in November. Dylan's 1964 hit "The Times They Are a-Changing," seemed to be an almost prophetic view of the power young protesters would exert over the next several years:

Come mothers and fathers throughout the land
And don't criticize what you can't understand
Your sons and your daughters are beyond your command
Your old road is rapidly agin'
Please get out of the new one if you can't lend your hand
For the times they are a-changin'.

The British Invasion

A major change to rock and roll music in America would occur around this same time. In early 1964, a British rock group called the Beatles released their first single in the United States. "I Want to Hold Your Hand" rose quickly to #1. The music the Beatles played was new and exciting, and it created an enormous enthusiasm among young people, known as "Beatlemania." In February 1964, the Beatles appeared on the *Ed Sullivan Show*. An estimated 70 million people watched that show, which was the largest audience in TV history to that point. Their appearance is considered a turning point in American culture.

The Beatles had an incredible impact on American popular music. They dominated the American music charts during 1964 and 1965, and nearly every song they released was a hit. Their success also helped other British artists get noticed in America.

To see the Beatles perform on the **Ed Sullivan Show** *in 1964, scan here:*

The Rolling Stones, Dusty Springfield, the Animals, the Dave Clark Five, and Herman's Hermits all had songs that hit #1 on the American pop charts by the end of 1965. Thanks to the wave of British groups that became popular in this time, the period is often called the "British Invasion."

The British Invasion affected more than just rock music. The Beatles and other British artists influenced the culture, clothing, and hair styles for an entire generation of young Americans. "It was a sweet surrender," recalls music journalist Parke Putterbaugh, "as millions of kids (and not a few adults) succumbed to the sound of guitar-wielding, mop-topped redcoats playing rock & roll that was fresh, exotically foreign and full of the vitality of a new age in the making."

Although none of the British rock groups would prove to be as popular as the Beatles, some came close. Compared to the clean-cut Beatles, the Rolling Stones cultivated a bad-boy image. The band had many top-40 hits during the 1960s, including #1 hits

Rolling Stones singer Mick Jagger and guitarist Keith Richards created such rock anthems as "(I Can't Get No) Satisfaction," "Jumpin' Jack Flash," and "Honky Tonk Women."

like "Get Off of My Cloud," "Ruby Tuesday," and "Paint it Black." During the 1970s, the Stones dominated the rock album charts, placing eight consecutive albums at #1 on the US charts. The Rolling Stones have continued making great rock music; in 2019 the band was still performing to sold-out stadium audiences.

The Beatles Meet Bob Dylan

In 1964, Bob Dylan was on tour in England, when he was introduced to the Beatles: John Lennon, Paul McCartney, George Harrison, and Ringo Starr. Their meeting would changed the landscape of rock and roll. Dylan soon traded his acoustic guitar for an electric guitar, and began recording music that was more like rock. This shocked and angered many folk music fans, but Dylan didn't care. "It was obvious to me that they had staying power," Dylan later said of the Beatles. "I knew they were pointing the direction that music had to go."

Dylan and the Beatles were also part of bringing drug use into the mainstream of rock and roll. Some accounts say Dylan introduced the Beatles to marijuana when they met in 1965. Drugs like marijuana, cocaine, and heroin had been used by musicians for decades. The Beatles and Dylan began making more overt references to drugs in their songs, and other artists began copying them. Using drugs was seen as a way of understanding deeper truths, and it was a way of not conforming to society's rules, which was also important in the youth culture of the 1960s.

Mikal Gilmore believes that the Beatles and Bob Dylan helped each other develop professionally, in ways they probably did not even imagine. The Beatles helped Dylan to make popular music that would appeal to young people outside of the traditional folk music audience. Dylan showed the Beatles that their music could be a way to discuss important issues and influence their audience. "Combined, the Beatles and Dylan had a seismic effect on popular music and youth culture," Gilmore wrote. "They changed the soundscape and ambition of rock and roll in thorough and irrevocable ways that … still carry tremendous influence."

The Motown Sound

While Dylan and the Beatles were changing the rock music landscape, a new style of music was developing in Detroit. In 1960, a songwriter and music producer named Berry Gordy Jr. spent $800 to start his own record label, which he called Motown Records. Over the next decade, Motown Records would become the largest black-owned business of any kind in the United States.

Both whites and black audiences loved the "Motown sound," which featured ear-catching melodies, powerful bass lines, an abundance of horns, and strong percussion sections. Motown lyrics were polished, yet catchy.

To an extent never before seen, Motown achieved crossover success with African-American music. Motown's artists notched numerous chart-topping hits and sold millions upon millions of records. Some of the most successful Motown artists included Smokey Robinson and the Miracles, Diana Ross and the Supremes, the Four Tops, the Temptations, Marvin Gaye, Stevie Wonder, Gladys Knight and the Pips, the Jackson Five, and Michael Jackson.

The popularity of the Motown sound reflected progress in the battle for racial equality. "I would come to the South in the early days of Motown and the audiences would be segregated," recalled Smokey Robinson. "Then they started to get the Motown music and we would go back and the audiences were integrated and the kids were dancing together and holding hands." A song like Aretha Franklin's 1967 hit "Respect," which spoke of both feminist and black pride, would never have been played on American radio stations even ten years earlier.

Berry Gordy started Motown Records in his home in Detroit in 1960. The label released more than 180 songs that hit #1 on the music charts, and influenced many genres of music, from rock to hip-hop.

Drugs, Hippies, and the Summer of Love

Late in the 1960s, new sounds started dominating rock and roll. Rock stars were openly using drugs and letting the substances influence their music. It was the era of "psychedelic rock," featuring long and loud instrumental riffs and lyrics about the effects of drug use. The music was also known as "acid rock," after a nickname for the psychedelic drug known as LSD ("acid"). Important groups from this era included the Grateful Dead and Jefferson Airplane, both of which got their starts in the Haight-Ashbury district of San Francisco, California.

Like other forms of rock, psychedelic music left its imprint on **pop culture**. Some young people sought freedom from the restrictions and expectations of American society. They became known as Hippies. Boys grew their hair long and stopped shaving. Clothes featured wild and colorful patterns. Kids went barefoot, stopped bathing, and talked about "flower power."

The peace sign became a familiar symbol in America, owing to the opposition of many young people to the war in Vietnam. More than 500,000 American soldiers were serving in Vietnam, and public opposition to the war was growing. Many rock musicians used their platform to speak out against the war, and at times rock music was caught in the crosshairs of what was becoming a full-blown cultural war.

In 1967, Hippies gathered all over the country, especially in San Francisco. They called for a "Summer of Love." A rock **music festival** in Monterey, California, attracted tens of thousands of people. The Grateful Dead and Jefferson Airplane both performed there. So did the Who, a rock band that had been popular in Britain, but was little known in the United States before the festival. The Who would go on to become one of America's favorite rock groups during the late 1960s and 1970s.

Jimi Hendrix was another artist who would gain fame and attention at the Monterey Pop Festival. Hendrix is widely regarded as the best rock guitarist of all time. He taught himself how to play, and his style was unique and innovative. He pioneered the use of feedback on the electric guitar. However, his career was brief. Only three studio albums, all with his trio the Jimi Hendrix Experience, were released during his lifetime. But those albums—*Are You Experienced* (1967), Axis: *Bold as Love* (1967), and *Electric Ladyland* (1968)—were hugely influential.

Perhaps the most important record released during the Summer of Love was *Sgt. Pepper's Lonely Hearts Club Band*, by the Beatles. The previous year, the band had decided to stop touring. They preferred to spend time in the recording studio,

A young anti-war demonstrator offers a flower to a military policeman during a 1967 rally to protest against the Vietnam War.

FREE YAWF LEADERS
JAILED FOR AIDING
ANTI-WAR G.I.'s

The grave of Jim Morrison, lead singer of the American rock band the Doors, is located in Paris, where the singer died of a heroin overdose in 1971. Morrison was among many rock stars who died from drugs or alcohol in the late 1960s and early 1970s. Others included Rolling Stones founder Brian Jones, singer Janice Joplin, and guitar virtuoso Jimi Hendrix.

coming up with imaginative sounds. *Sgt. Pepper's Lonely Hearts Club Band* was artsy and provocative. Even the record's packaging was covered with art. The music was edgy and brilliant. *Sgt. Pepper's Lonely Hearts Club Band* is often listed as the greatest rock album of all time.

In August 1969, another major rock music festival was held at Woodstock. The free festival, held on a rural New York farm, lasted for three days. Woodstock was a major statement of youth culture in the 1960s. Approximately 400,000 people came to enjoy the music. Bob Dylan performed at Woodstock, and so did folk singers Joan Baez and Arlo Guthrie. Rock bands that performed included the Grateful Dead, Jefferson Airplane, and Creedence Clearwater Revival. And Jimi Hendrix's searing rendition of "The Star-Spangled Banner" became the stuff of musical legend.

Continuing to Change

By the end of the 1960s, the rock musician had become an artist in his or her own right. No longer limited to just singing simple songs, the musicians now were artists, using studio technologies and additional instrumentation to create complex and powerful music. Making political and social statements also became the norm.

Albums were the means through which messages were sent, and creating cohesive albums filled with good music became more important to many artists than releasing hit singles. A paradox was developing. The artist-musician expressed disdain for the music charts that reflected his or her popularity. Sales of albums and concert tickets were at an all-time high.

It was during this time that the tendency to split "rock and roll" music from "rock" music originated. "Rock and roll" often referred to singles that were released in hopes of getting airplay on AM radio stations, and rising up *Billboard's* Hot 100 or Top 40 charts. "Rock" referred to album music played by FM stations, which were not as popular as AM radio at the time. Rock was considered "authentic" in that it promoted the idea of personal and communal experience between the artist and the fans. Rock and roll became softer and more like pop music, while rock became louder.

Thus the late 1960s set the stage for a further blossoming of rock and roll. It had been a mixture of many styles and now was set to give birth to many new styles itself.

TEXT-DEPENDENT QUESTIONS

1. What was the California surf sound?
2. Which rock groups were at the forefront of the British Invasion?
3. When was the Summer of Love?

 # RESEARCH PROJECT

Do some research on blues musicians of the late 1950s. Read about them touring Europe before the Beatles and the British Invasion started. Write a paper about what could be called a counter-invasion. How did those blues musicians affect the British Invasion that came later.

Robert Plant and Jimmy Page of Led Zeppelin perform during the band's 1975 tour of North America. Page is playing an unusual double-neck guitar, which enabled him to perform intricate songs like "Stairway to Heaven" without having to switch instruments.

 WORDS TO UNDERSTAND

androgynous—having both male and female characteristics.

music video—a short film made to accompany a song, usually intended to promote the sale of the music.

subgenre—a category or type of something within a larger genre.

suburbanite—a person who lives in the suburbs, residential communities that are outside of the cities.

CHAPTER 4

Rock Matures

Rock music reached a level of maturity in the 1970s and 1980s. It was still youth driven, but had become the most popular type of music in the United States and in much of Europe. The "classic rock" era featured star performers like the Rolling Stones, the Doors, Steely Dan, Santana, Creedence Clearwater Revival, Joni Mitchell, the Steve Miller Band, Bruce Springsteen, and Crosby, Stills, Nash, and Young cranking out amazing albums. Artists experimented with musical styles, and rock splintered into many new forms.

Singer/songwriters like Paul Simon and Art Garfunkel, James Taylor, Jackson Brown, Carole King, Cat Stevens, and others were rooted in the folk music of the 1960s. Their music was aimed at middle-class white **suburbanites**. Bands like England Dan and John Ford Coley, Air Supply, Seals and Crofts, and America also played more gentle, melodic rock songs that were hits. They focused on releasing hit singles, rather than on cohesive albums. This "soft rock" was much different than the "hard rock" made popular by groups like Led Zeppelin, Aerosmith, Foghat, and KISS. This type of music is sometimes called "adult contemporary" or "easy listening."

One band that found amazing success with a softer, more pop-oriented rock music sound was Fleetwood Mac. The band had originally formed in Britain to play blues-rock, achieving only modest success in the early 1970s. But in 1974, when guitarist Lindsey Buckingham and vocalist Stevie Nicks joined Fleetwood Mac, the band took off. Their 1975 album *Fleetwood Mac* was a #1 hit in the United States. Their 1977 album *Rumors* did even better, spawning four top-10 singles and becoming the best-selling album of the decade. However, the band members did not get along well, and had many disagreements. These would eventually cause Fleetwood Mac to break up, although the band would remain an important musical force until the late 1980s.

 ## BEYOND THE BEATLES

The Beatles broke up in 1970, but each of the four band members continued to play and had excellent solo careers. John Lennon recorded songs with his wife, Yoko Ono, and released hits like "Imagine" and "(Just Like) Starting Over." Paul McCartney also teamed up with his wife, Linda Eastman McCartney, to form the band Wings. Their 1973 album *Band on the Run* was a #1 hit in the United States and the United Kingdom, and they released many singles that hit the top-40 charts. In 1970 George Harrison released an unusual "triple album" (three records of music) called *All Things Must Pass*, which contained several hits and is considered a masterpiece. And drummer Ringo Starr charted eight top-10 hits and also began a career acting in movies.

Fleetwood Mac was one of the most influential rock groups of the 1970s. The band members drew on their personal problems to create enduring hits.

Billy Joel was another successful pop-rock musician. He had several top-10 hits before releasing his breakthrough album, *The Stranger*, in 1977. During his twenty-year career, Joel would have thirty-three hits in the top-40, including three that reached #1.

Groups like Led Zeppelin played a very different style of rock music. Led Zeppelin was an English rock band that had formed in the late 1960s. The band started out playing a blend of blues and rock music, to which they added elements of psychedelic rock and folk music. They created heavy-hitting songs that featured intricate guitar solos by Jimmy Page, as well as pounding drum interludes by John Bonham. Vocalist Robert Plant had a distinctive voice and could hit amazing high notes, and bass player/keyboardist John Paul Jones provided a solid rhythmic foundation. Over an eleven-year period, Led Zeppelin released eight successful albums, selling millions of copies. Although Led Zeppelin's most popular song, "Stairway to Heaven," was never released as a single, it would become the most-played song on FM radio stations during the 1970s.

Most music critics compare Led Zeppelin's influence on the direction of rock music during the 1970s to the impact of the Beatles in the 1960s. The band inspired a host of imitators, and helped to create the hard rock and heavy metal **subgenres** of rock music.

Hard Rock

Hard rock music is very energetic and is fueled by loud guitars. The guitars often used an amplifier effect called distortion, that produced a fuzzy tone. Vocals were screamed or shouted, and the bass and drum rhythms were strong and driving. Rock bands like the Who began performing songs with this heavier sound during the 1970s.

The Australian rock band AC/DC was formed in 1973 by brothers Malcolm and Angus Young. They had several hits during the 1970s, but broke through to mainstream popularity with their 1980 album *Back in Black*, one of the bestselling rock albums of all time. Among AC/DC's most popular songs are "It's a Long Way to the Top if you Wanna Rock and Roll" and "Thunderstruck."

Queen was a band that was difficult to label. While their music falls into the category of hard rock, the band members were incredibly talented and experimented with many forms of music. Lead vocalist Freddie Mercury was famous for the range of his voice. Other band members included guitarist Brian May, drummer Roger Taylor, and bass guitarist John Deacon. Their early hit "Bohemian Rhapsody" was a #1 hit in the United Kingdom. It was one of the first songs for which a promotional film, called **music video**, was created. The band had many top-40

Portrait of rock star Freddy Mercury, whose distinctive voice and flamboyant personality helped the band Queen to sell millions of albums during the 1970s and early 1980s. The rock star's life was chronicled in the 2018 film Bohemian Rhapsody.

hits in the United States, including the #1 hits "Crazy Little Thing Called Love" and "Another One Bites the Dust," which blended rock with the driving beat of disco dance music.

Rock audiences enjoyed the antics of KISS, whose members created elaborate face-painted personas. Their live performances

Kiss members in their band personas— Gene Simmons as "the Demon," Paul Stanley as "the Starchild," and Tommy Thayer as "the Spaceman"— during a concert.

featured band members breathing fire, drum sets that floated above the stage, smoke, and fireworks. Fans loved the band's hard-rock hits like "Detroit Rock City" and "Rock and Roll All Night."

One of KISS's biggest contributions to rock music may have been the introduction of the "power ballad." The 1976 song "Beth" does not sound like any other KISS song. The vocals by Peter Criss are backed by piano and a string orchestra, not guitars and drums. The band didn't even want to include it on their album, because it was so unlike their usual music. But "Beth" became the band's biggest hit. Soon, it seemed like every other hard rock group was including a power ballad on their own albums, such as Nazareth's "Love Hurts," Journey's "Faithfully," and Guns N' Roses's "November Rain."

Aerosmith was one of the most popular bands of the 1970s, with a string of hits like "Sweet Emotion," "Dream On," and "Walk This Way." But drug addiction and disagreements among the band members derailed the group from the late 1970s to late 1980s. Aerosmith would make a comeback in the 1990s that would see the band becoming even more successful. The group had many top-40 hits, including its first #1 hit in 1998, the power ballad "I Don't Want to Miss a Thing."

The unusual guitar-playing style of Eddie Van Halen contributed to the distinctive sound of the band he formed with his brother Alex, a drummer. Van Halen formed in the mid-1970s, and by the early 1980s they were one of the most successful rock acts of the time. After their record *1984* sold more than 10 million copies, lead singer David Lee Roth left for a solo career. The band brought in singer Sammy Hagar to replace him, and continued releasing hit albums. Van Halen has had thirteen songs hit #1 on *Billboard's* Mainstream Rock charts.

Heavy Metal, Glam, and Hair Metal

In the early 1970s, a few groups took the hard rock approach even further, developing a sound known as heavy metal. Guitars were even more distorted and louder, and the music even more dense and "heavy." Instead of songs about romantic love or fun times, heavy metal lyrics were more ominous, focusing on war, violence, or death. Some songs were about current affairs or

Pyrotechnics and light shows are often an important element of heavy metal concerts. This is a show by the groundbreaking metal band Metallica in California.

historical events. Others were about the supernatural, such as demons or devils.

Early heavy metal groups included Judas Priest and Black Sabbath. Others that were successful include Mötley Crüe, Pantera, and Megadeth. Metallica became known for its aggressive, high tempo songs, which were sometimes called "thrash." Their 1986 album *Master of Puppets* drew many new fans to the heavy metal genre. The band has been very successful, selling millions of albums and winning nine Grammy Awards.

Around the same time, a style of music called "glam rock" became popular, first in England and then spreading to the United States. Performers wore lavish makeup and exotic sequined outfits, creating an **androgynous** look. Rock musicians like Freddy Mercury of Queen or the hard rock band KISS included "glam" elements in their performances.

David Bowie was among the most famous and successful. He created a flamboyant persona called Ziggy Stardust in the mid-1970s, and performed concerts to sold-out crowds. Bowie was a very talented musician, and would experiment with many different styles of rock music during his long career.

Elton John was another rock star who found success with the glam style. He co-wrote many hits with lyricist Bernie Taupin, including "Crocodile Rock" and "Bennie and the Jets." In all, Elton John had fifty-seven songs hit the top-40 in the United States, including nine that reached #1. In 1997, he re-recorded an earlier hit, "Candle in the Wind," as a tribute to Britain's beloved Diana, princess of Wales, who had been killed in a car accident. The song would sell more than 33 million copies, becoming the best-selling single of all time.

In the 1980s, some groups blended heavy metal sounds with glam sensibility to create "hair metal." Unlike heavy metal, the lyrics were intended to appeal to pop audiences. Bands like Quiet Riot, Def Leppard, Bon Jovi, Poison, Cinderella, and Warrant were popular from the mid-1980s into the 1990s.

Punk rock fans showed their opposition to society's conventions by dressing in ways that some people felt were shocking: body piercings and tattoos, unusual hairstyles featuring bright colors, and black leather jackets with heavy boots, ornamented with chains and safety pins.

Progressive, Punk, and Industrial

Some groups wanted to expand the boundaries of rock music beyond the usual format of three or four minutes per song that radio stations preferred. Their music became known as progressive rock. Progressive rock groups were inspired by the more experimental later work of the Beatles, as well as the long jams of the Grateful Dead. They created concept albums, in which all of the songs related to a predetermined theme. They used orchestra instruments and synthesizers to create different sounds. The groups began to conduct lavish concerts, with lasers and light shows to highlight the music.

A British group called Pink Floyd had experienced modest success in the 1960s, but the band's popularity took off during the 1970s. They blended psychedelic elements and extensive studio work, and each album explored important themes, such as isolation, greed, the price of fame, and mental illness. *The Dark Side of the Moon* (1973) became one of the best-selling rock albums of all time. It was followed by *Wish You Were Here* (1975), *Animals* (1977), and *The Wall* (1979). Throughout the decade, Pink Floyd's concerts became more ambitious. A stage show was created for a concert tour to promote *The Wall*, and eventually turned into a popular movie. Other progressive groups that experimented with sound and the rock music form during the 1970s and 1980s included the Moody Blues, Electric Light Orchestra, Jethro Tull, King Crimson, Yes, and Genesis.

Another important movement within rock music during this time was among bands who wanted to strip away the polished studio production of the music. Punk rock bands wanted to return to a simplified form of rock music, with loud guitars and plenty of attitude. Most punk songs were short, and played at a very fast tempo.

A British band called the Sex Pistols was among the first to make punk rock popular. The raw energy of their 1977 album *Never Mind the Bollocks, Here's the Sex Pistols* inspired many other punk groups, both in Britain and in America. Songs like "Anarchy in the UK" and "God Save the Queen" criticized and made fun of British government and social conventions. Other punk groups, such as the Clash and the Ramones, would also express this attitude toward society.

Punk musicians, as well as their fans, soon created their own culture of opposition to government and social rules. They wore shirts that contained offensive sayings, leather jackets, ripped clothing, and Dr. Martens boots. Some got extensive tattoos, or wore garish jewelry. Hairstyles often involved bright colors and unusual forms, such as the spiked mohawk.

CHANGING TECHNOLOGY

As in every era, technological changes were important to the development of rock music in the 1970s and 1980s. Prior to the 1970s, most people listened to record albums at their homes, and to the radio when in the car. The development of music cassette tapes and "eight-track" tapes made music more portable. People could play their music in the car, or on portable tape players that they could carry with them wherever they went. Also, in the 1980s the compact disc, or CD, began to replace the vinyl record as the most popular format for music albums. CDs could hold more music, and the quality of the sound was much better than the vinyl albums.

Another form of music, called "industrial rock," also evolved from punk music. It used different kinds of instruments and used things not normally thought of as instruments, to make music. Some bands that found success in this style were Nine Inch Nails and Marilyn Manson.

Music Television

In 1981, a cable television channel called MTV, for "music television," was launched. At first, MTV just played short films, or videos, that music groups created to promote their songs. The early videos usually just contained scenes of the band or musician playing, but soon the music video took an artistic life in itself. Videos became musical theater, adding a new dimension to rock and roll.

Nobody understood the relationship between music and video better than Michael Jackson. In 1982, he recorded the album *Thriller*. The record, which blended R&B, rock, and dance music, took off like a rocket. Within two years, it sold a stunning 40 million copies, and nine of its 10 songs made the *Billboard* top-10 list. Videos that starred Jackson singing and dancing to the songs from the album were played over and over again on MTV. They helped boost *Thriller's* sales. In turn the success of the album helped to make MTV an important force in the music industry.

The success of *Thriller* and the popularity of MTV made it essentially required for rock artists to create music videos to accompany their songs. In 1984 Bruce Springsteen's album *Born in the USA* was released. His songs reflected the hardships and hope felt by many Americans, and the album soon became a best-seller. The Irish rock band U2 was introduced to many Americans by MTV. Other rock groups that attracted attention due to their videos included Van Halen, Billy Joel, John Mellencamp, Genesis, Def Leppard, Prince, and Bon Jovi.

Irish rock band U2 was one of the most popular and innovative groups of the 1980s and 1990s. The group's members are known for their work on humanitarian causes, particularly lead singer Bono (second from left).

New Wave and Post Punk

The creation of MTV made music available to more people than ever before. It also created opportunities for more musicians. Punk rock was fading, but keyboard-driven bands created a post-punk wave with an introverted songwriting style. This was called New Wave.

Many New Wave groups relied on the vibrating sounds made by the synthesizer—an electronic device that could create a variety of artificial sounds. MTV promoted this new sound—the first song aired on the channel was "Video Killed the Radio Star," by a British New Wave group called the Buggles. Other New Wave groups that were popular in the 1980s included the Human League, A Flock of Seagulls, Eurythmics, Soft Cell, Depeche Mode, and Orchestral Maneuvers in the Dark (OMD).

Some artists played more conventional rock tunes, but infused them with the ironic attitude of punk rock. Some took a commercial, pop-rock approach, such as the Romantics, Cheap Trick, and Squeeze. Others played darker songs that were less appealing to a pop audience, such as the Cure, Siouxsie and the Banshees, or the Talking Heads.

While rock was splintering into many sub-genres, most people listened to all different kinds of rock music. MTV might play a song by Soft Cell and follow it with a Michael Jackson hit, and then a John Mellencamp song. Music fans related to each other and developed a sense of community. There seemed to be endless possibilities to create new rock music.

Rock Stars Give Back

In the 1960s, rock musicians had sung songs that protested the Vietnam War and other government policies. During the 1970s and 1980s, rock stars began taking a more active role in working for the causes they believed in. One way that people who had become wealthy through their music could help others was by performing charity concerts.

One of the first high profile event was held by former Beatle George Harrison in 1971. He wanted to help people in Bangladesh, a country in South Asia that was fighting a war for independence from Pakistan. The people of Bangladesh were suffering from the war, as well as from a famine. Harrison's Concert for Bangladesh featured many of his friends from the music industry, including Ringo Star, Bob Dylan, Eric Clapton, Billy Preston, and the band Badfinger. The initial concert raised $250,000. But the promoters also made an album of music as well as a film of the event, and profits from those projects—estimated at $12 million—was sent to Bangladesh.

In 1984, a group of British rock stars led by Bob Geldof (of the band Boomtown Rats) recorded the song "Do They Know It's Christmas?" to help raise money and awareness for the people of Ethiopia, who were suffering from a terrible famine. The song raised over $10 million for charity. The next year, many of the most popular American rock stars got together to record "We Are the World." That song was a #1 hit, raising over $60 million for humanitarian aid to Africa.

In July 1985, Geldof helped to organize a series of rock concerts called Live Aid, to raise money for Africa and awareness of problems on that continent. The biggest concerts were in London and Philadelphia, but there were smaller concerts in other countries as well. They featured some of the time's biggest stars, including Queen, Tom Petty, Mick Jagger, Madonna, the Beach Boys, and the Who. Billions of people around the world watched the shows on television. Live Aid eventually raised more than $125 million for Africa.

Scan here to see Neil Young sing at Farm Aid in 1986:

Jon Bon Jovi performs at the Live 8 concert in Philadelphia. The 2005 charity event drew approximately a million rock music fans.

The success of Live Aid inspired some American musicians to create a similar event to help farmers, who were struggling due to low crop prices and high mortgage costs. In 1986, Willie Nelson, John Mellencamp, Neil Young, and others organized Farm Aid. The event raised over $9 million for American family farmers that year, and continues to be held regularly.

Other rock stars have embraced similar causes. A 1985 recording of "That's What Friends are For" by Dionne Warwick, Gladys Knight, Elton John, and Stevie Wonder raised $3 million for AIDS research. In 2005, a series of ten concerts were held simultaneously in cities around the world. Known as Live 8, they raised millions to combat global poverty. And in 2012, Bruce Springsteen, the Who, Eric Clapton, Billy Joel, and other major rock acts performed at the Concert for Sandy Relief, raising more than $30 million to help people in New York and New Jersey who had lost their homes due to Hurricane Sandy earlier that year.

TEXT-DEPENDENT QUESTIONS

1. What was Glam Rock?
2. How did MTV change the way music was marketed?
3. What was the purpose of the 1985 Live Aid concerts?

RESEARCH PROJECT

Visit the Rock and Roll Hall of Fame website. Look through the list of inductees, and choose one of them. Read some more about that musician or group, and listen to their music. Then write a short paper about the artist, and why they belong in a rock music hall of fame.

Greta Van Fleet's first album Anthem of the Peaceful Army, *released in 2018, topped the* Billboard *rock album chart.*

 # WORDS TO UNDERSTAND

disillusionment—a feeling of disappointment resulting from the discovery that something is not as good as one hoped it would be.

file-sharing program—a program that allows digital media, such as music files or videos, to be accessed by computers connected to a network.

music-streaming service—a way of delivering music over the Internet, without requiring the listener to download files to their computer or device.

CHAPTER 5

Rock and Roll Is Here to Stay

The growth of rock and roll has been phenomenal. While some say it is in decline, others say it is more vibrant than ever. The expansion of the *Billboard* charts reflects how rock and roll has developed and changed over the years.

Billboard magazine began publishing its chart of the Hot 100 songs in 1958. The list was based on sales and radio play, and it was the only list of popular music. Rock songs still appear on the Hot 100, but today *Billboard* publishes dozen of charts, including many specifically for the category of rock music. These include Hot Rock Songs, Rock Airplay, Top Rock Albums, Alternative Songs, Mainstream Rock Songs, and Hard Rock Albums, among others. There are many other ways to track the popularity of songs as well: measuring store sales, radio play, internet streaming, video streaming, and other categories.

Today there are many different kinds of rock music. There is also technology that has changed the music world. Today's music is not limited to people playing an instrument and singing. Some music is made electronically, without the use of traditional instruments. Thanks to improved technology, the small independent recording company is also making a comeback. Almost anyone can start an "Indie" record company and produce rock songs.

Alternative Rock

In the late 1980s, a new form of rock music emerged. The music expressed independence of spirit and a do-it-yourself attitude, mixed with the attitude and loud guitars of punk rock. It was billed as an alternative to mainstream rock and roll, but by the end of the decade it was the most popular form of rock. In that sense, Alternative Rock became mainstream, and mainstream became something else.

Many alternative bands got their start with small independent recording studios, and first appealed to regional audiences. The band REM from Georgia was one of the first Alternative bands to reach the mainstream. The band had been popular with college audiences for nearly a decade, before scoring a top-10 hit with "The One I Love" in 1987. This success enabled REM to leave the small IRS Records label and sign with a major company, Warner Brothers Records. The band would release several successful albums over the next decade, and the song "Losing My Religion" (1991) would hit #4 on the Hot 100 chart.

Other Alternative groups that were successful in the 1980s included two bands from Minneapolis, Hüsker Dü and the Replacements. Another band, They Might Be Giants, played songs with unusual and creative lyrics. Their third album, *Flood* (1989) sold more than a million copies and included the hit single "Birdhouse in Your Soul," which reached #3 on the Modern Rock chart.

Radiohead had great success, as well as Coldplay, as their alternative sound became mainstream rock and roll. Radiohead moved away from experimental music in the 2000s, while Coldplay had four #1 albums in the United States. The British indie rock scene came back later in the decade with bands like the Arctic Monkeys and Franz Ferdinand.

Alternative rock continues to be popular among young people. By 2018 newer bands like Avenged Sevenfold, Arcade Fire, Queens of the Stone Age, Kings of Leon, and Alter Bridge were

among the most popular American rock performers.

Grunge and Post-Grunge

The band Nirvana brought a new style of alternative music into the mainstream in the 1990s. The Grunge sound originated in Seattle, among bands like Soundgarden, Alice in Chains, and Pearl Jam. The music was loud, while the lyrics were often ironic and offering little hope for a rosy future. They reflected the **disillusionment** of young members of "Generation X," the post-Baby Boom generation, who had grown up in the 1980s and come of age

Josh Dun and Tyler Joseph of Twenty One Pilots attend an MTV Video Music Awards ceremony. The alternative band's 2015 album Blurryface *included two hit singles, "Stressed Out" and "Ride."*

during a time of economic problems and high unemployment in the United States. Grunge fans did not want to be flashy. They dressed in flannel shirts and ripped jeans.

Nirvana's first album, *Nevermind* (1991), included several hit singles, such as "Smells Like Teen Spirit" and "Come As You Are." The songs used heavy guitar riffs and dark, gloomy lyrics. It reached #1 on the *Billboard* Top 200 Albums chart, an amazing accomplishment for an Alternative band, and eventually sold over 20 million copes. *Nevermind* would attract new fans to Grunge music. However, the pressures of fame would lead Nirvana's lead singer, Kurt Cobain, to commit suicide in 1994.

The Foo Fighters—Nate Mendel, Dave Grohl, Taylor Hawkins, Chris Shiflett, and Pat Smear—attend a 2012 event. The post-grunge band has been one of the most successful rock groups of the twenty-first century.

Pearl Jam was one of the best-selling rock bands of the 1990s, thanks to their hit albums *Ten* (1991), *Vs* (1993), and *Vitalogy* (1994). Their records included top-10 hits like "Alive," "Jeremy," and "Daughter." Pearl Jam lyrics were often dark and brooding, accompanied with powerful harmonic rock riffs. Like Nirvana, the members of Pearl Jam seemed uncomfortable with their fame. Singer Eddie Vedder and other band members did not want to make videos or give interviews, they just wanted to play their music. But they also became upset when the enormous Ticketmaster corporation added extra fees to the cost of Pearl Jam concert tickets. The band wanted to ensure that fans could afford to see them play, so they refused to play concerts in

Ticketmaster-controlled arenas. Eventually, however, Pearl Jam had to end this policy, because Ticketmaster controlled most of the major stadiums where rock concerts were held.

After Cobain's death and the breakup of Nirvana, the band's drummer Dave Grohl created a new group, the Foo Fighters. The group has been very successful. Since 1995, four of the Foo Fighters' nine albums have won Grammy Awards for Best Rock Album. In 2017, their album *Concrete and Gold* hit #1 on the *Billboard* album chart. "We all love music, whether it's the Beatles or Queen or punk rock," Grohl once told an interviewer when talking about his musical influences. "I think the lure of punk rock was the energy and immediacy; the need to thrash stuff around. But at the same time, we're all suckers for a beautiful melody, you know? So it is just natural."

The Foo Fighters' sound, which blended the dark lyrics and strong riffs of grunge with a more melodic rock style, helped to usher in a "post-grunge" sound in the 2000s. Bands like Nickleback, Creed, and Matchbox Twenty maintained the attitude and guitar sounds of grunge, but their songs were more polished so they would appeal to pop audiences.

The Internet and Napster

During the 1990s, personal computers and the Internet began changing the world. The digital revolution has profoundly affected the music industry. Records, cassette tapes, and CDs made music available to everyone. But they also made it possible for record companies to control what music was sold, and to make a profit from the sale of every album or single. Computers and the Internet took power away from the record companies and gave it to listeners.

In the late 1990s, computer software was created that enabled people to copy their CDs onto a computer. They could play back the digital file, or "burn" the music files onto a new CD. This meant a person could buy an album and give inexpensive

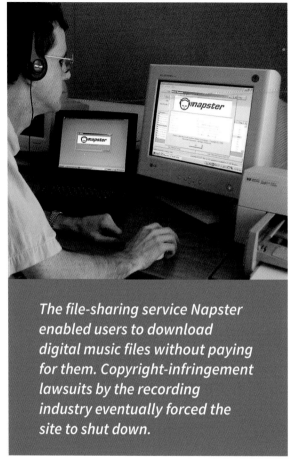

The file-sharing service Napster enabled users to download digital music files without paying for them. Copyright-infringement lawsuits by the recording industry eventually forced the site to shut down.

copies to their friends.

In 2000, a **file-sharing program** called Napster was invented by two teenagers. The program allowed digital music files to be shared between computers located all over the world. It allowed someone in Kansas, for example, to download a song or album that someone owned in Australia.

"It's difficult to describe to people . . . how much material was suddenly available," commented John Perry Barlow, a poet and technology guru. "There was no ramp up. There was no transition. It was like that famous shot from *2001: A Space Odyssey*, when the prehistoric monkey throws a bone in the air and it turns into a spaceship. Napster was a ridiculous leap forward."

Suddenly, people had access to all sorts of music—and they didn't have to pay for it. This of course meant fewer people were buying CDs, and less profit for the record companies and the musicians themselves. Soon there were more than 2 million people using file-sharing services like Napster. The music industry acted quickly and through the courts managed to shut down Napster and other file-sharing services.

The Record Industry Association of America (RIAA) sued Napster, as well as a few thousand people who had downloaded music through the service. They were sued for violating copyright laws. The RIAA won judgements against the people who had downloaded music. However, Napster had only provided a way for people to share the files. It had no music files stored on servers, and never provided music files to others.

Napster eventually closed down, but digital music was here to stay. Sales of CDs and other formats would never recover to their pre-2000 levels. New services, such as Apple's iTunes Music Store, were soon created, allowing people to download songs for a small fee. Eventually, music streaming services such as Spotify or Pandora enabled people can listen to music for free, and pay to download songs that they liked. By 2018, **music-streaming services** accounted for 75 percent of music industry revenue, according to *Rolling Stone*. As many as a million new people become stream service users each month.

The staying power of music has also changed drastically since the advent of the Internet. In times past, pre-Internet, a top album could stay on the charts for a few months, and a great one could stay there much of a year. Now albums get to the top fast, and fall away just as fast. In 1998, seventeen albums held the #1 place on the rock music charts. Twenty years later, in 2018, more than forty different albums reached the top of the charts.

Getting the Message Out

The Internet made it possible for unknown musicians to gain fans and sell their music in a way that they never could previously. During the early 2000s, an early form of social media called Myspace was popular, particularly among musicians. The site was very popular among teens and young adults, especially from 2004 until about 2010. Music groups could upload their songs to the site, where others could hear them. The Arctic Monkeys, an English rock band, and Ice Nine Kills, a heavy metal band from Boston, are among many artists that gained their first exposure through Myspace.

More recently, YouTube has enabled artists to upload their songs and videos, which can be liked and shared by music fans. Many of today's music stars were first noticed through their YouTube submissions, including the rockers 5 Seconds of Summer and Ed Sheeran, as well as rock-influenced pop stars like Justin Bieber and Charlie Puth.

The Internet enables musicians from all over the world to get noticed. A Mongolian heavy metal band called the Hu recently received more than seven million views of two songs it released on YouTube according to a recent NPR article. The group uses traditional Mongolian guttural singing to accompany its heavy metal rock. In addition to the usual guitars and drums, a member of the band plays a fiddle-like Mongolian instrument called a *morin khuur*. The result is unique-sounding metal music. "Mongolians are not just taking elements from Western music and just copying and pasting," explains Thalea Stokes, a student of ethnic music at the University of Chicago. "Instead, they're using some of these elements and making their own authentic music. So it's not rock music performed by Mongolians. It's Mongolian rock music."

But older technologies remain important as well. Radio stations had made musicians famous when rock and roll began in the 1950s, and they still play an important role in that today. In 2018, 228 million Americans said that they still listened to music on the radio more than once a week. About half of them said they found new music through listening to the radio. Only 27 percent said they found new music online, such as through streaming services. Radio remains a potent force in the fortunes of rock and roll musicians.

Scan here for music by the Hu,
a Mongolian heavy metal band:

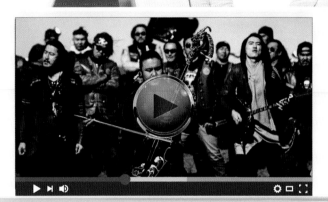

Many Faces of Rock

The Internet has changed the way music is distributed, and how musicians can promote themselves. But some things have not changed. Some of the rock musicians of the 1960s are still performing. Bob Dylan, who helped to change popular music in the 1960s, received the Nobel Prize for Literature in 2017, and announced plans for a European tour in 2019. Paul McCartney has continued creating new music, and in 2018 his album *Egypt Station* hit #1 on the *Billboard* 200 album chart. The Rolling Stones are also still touring and releasing albums of new music. Bands like the Allman Brothers, Lynyrd Skynyrd, and Creedence Clearwater Revival may have only a few of their original members left, but they are still playing their older songs—and often performing new rock compositions as well.

Elvis, the "king of rock and roll," has been dead since 1977, but his memory remains very much alive. His home in Memphis—Graceland—remains a popular tourist destination.

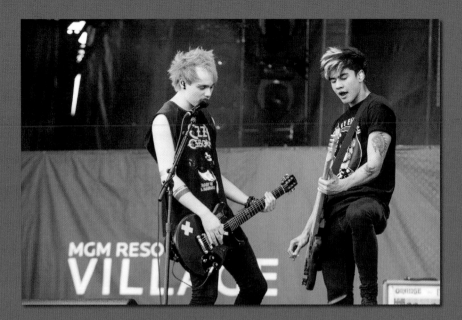

Lead guitarist Michael Clifford jams with bass guitarist Calum Hood during a 5 Seconds of Summer concert. The band from Australia originally attracted notice on YouTube, before being signed to a record deal. The group's first three albums all reached #1 in the United States.

There are also hundreds of Elvis impersonators, some of whom have a substantial following.

Bill Flanagan wrote in the *New York Times* in 2016, that rock and roll remains very much alive, even though many of the music's fans are older. The core of the rock music audience was born in the 1950s and 1960s, and they are still buying rock albums and concert tickets. According to Flanagan, the rock genre is where jazz was thirty years ago—fully developed, and now looking back at past glories. But while hip-hop music is more popular than rock among younger Americans, Flanagan does not see rock and roll disappearing, however. "Rock 'n' roll certainly is for old people now," he wrote. "It's for those young people who want it, too. Like any music that lasts, it's for anyone who cares to listen."

TEXT-DEPENDENT QUESTIONS

1. What are some elements of Alternative Rock?
2. What rock group did Dave Grohl start after the breakup of Nirvana?
3. How did the Internet impact rock music?

RESEARCH PROJECT

Using the Internet or your school library, find out more about Napster and the legal challenges that forced it to stop operating. Should people be allowed to share music they have purchased with others? Is it fair for record companies to say that such sharing is stealing? Write a one-page paper and share it with your class, using facts to support your your opinions on the matter.

SERIES GLOSSARY OF KEY TERMS

A&R department—the talent department at a record label, which is responsible for finding artists and acquiring songs for them to record. A&R stands for "artists and repertoire."

audio mixing—the process by which multiple sounds are combined into a finished song. The music producer often uses a mixing console to manipulate or enhance each source sound's volume and dynamics.

ballad—a folk song that narrates a story in short stanzas.

beat—the steady pulse that listeners feel in a musical piece.

bootleg—an unauthorized recording of a song.

chord—three or more tones played at the same time.

copyright—the exclusive legal right to control the publication or reproduction of artistic works, such as songs, books, or movies. Musicians protect their original songs through copyright to prevent other people from stealing their songs, lyrics, or musical tunes. The period of copyright protection is generally seventy years after the death of the creator of the work.

demo—short for "demonstration recording," a song that that is professionally produced and recorded to demonstrate the ability of a musician or musical group.

harmony—the simultaneous combination of tones or pitches, especially when blended into chords that are pleasing to the ear.

hook—the "catchy" part of a song that makes people want to hear it repeatedly. The hook can be lyrical or musical. It is often the title of the song, and is usually repeated frequently throughout the song.

hymn—a song of religious worship.

instrumentation—the way a song's composer or arranger assigns elements of the music to specific instruments. When done for an orchestra, this is called "orchestration."

lyrics—the words of a song.

mastering—the final process of preparing a mixed recording for commercial distribution.

measure—a way of organizing music according to its rhythmic structure. Each measure, or "bar," includes a certain number of beats.

pitch—term used to describe how high or low a note sounds. Pitch is determined by the note's frequency, or the number of complete oscillations per second of energy as sound in the form of sound-waves.

producer—the person in charge of making a record. Chooses the musicians, instrumentation, and songs for the project, and oversees it to completion, often in collaboration with the recording artist and staff of the record company.

riff—a short repeated phrase in popular music and jazz, typically used as an introduction or refrain in a song.

rhythm—a strong, regular, repeated pattern of musical sounds.

scale—a sequence of notes in either descending or ascending order.

signature song—a song that a popular music artist or band is most known for or associated with, usually one of their biggest hits. The most popular artists can have more than one signature song.

solo—a piece of music, or a passage in a piece of music, that is performed by one musician.

tempo—the speed at which a piece of music is played.

CHAPTER NOTES

CHAPTER 1

p. 11: "Rock & roll is nothing …" Fats Domino, quoted in Black Music Scholar, "Features of the 1950s," (accessed February 2019). https://blackmusicscholar.com/features-of-the-1950s/

p. 12: "Nobody—not Chuck Berry …" Richard Williams, "Sister Rosetta Tharp: The Godmother of Rock and Roll," *The Guardian* (March 18, 2015). https://www.theguardian.com/music/2015/mar/18/sister-rosetta-tharpe-gospel-singer-100th-birthday-tribute

p. 13: "brutally honest songs about his life …" Rock and Roll Hall of Fame and Museum, "Hank Williams," (1987). https://www.rockhall.com/inductees/hank-williamse

p. 14: "A mixture of white and black …" Gregory McNamee, "1948 and the Birth of Rock and Roll Music," *Encyclopedia Britannica* blog (January 22, 2008). http://blogs.britannica.com/2008/01/1948-and-the-birth-of-rock-and-roll-music/

p. 16: "Even though you'll find things …" Tony Cajiao, quoted in Alexis Petridis, "Will the Creator of Modern Music Please Stand Up," *The Guardia*n (April 16, 2004). https://www.theguardian.com/music/2004/apr/16/popandrock

p. 18: "The Graves brothers' …" Robert Palmer, quoted in Anthony DeCurtis et al., eds, The Rolling Stone Illustrated History of Rock and Roll (New York: Random House, 1992), p. 4.

CHAPTER 2

p. 21: "It was so much more …" Robert Palmer, "The 50s: A Decade of Music That Changed the World," *Rolling Stone* (April 19, 1990). https://www.rollingstone.com/music/music-features/the-50s-a-decade-of-music-that-changed-the-world-229924/

p. 24: "Everyone knew that I was …" Sun Records, biography of Sam Phillips (accessed February 2019). https://www.sunrecords.com/artists/sam-phillips

p. 30: "The 'Ace from Outer Space' …" Todd Leopold, "The Kings of the Radio: All-time Great DJs," CNN Entertainment (May 17, 2013). http://www.cnn.com/2013/05/17/showbiz/hfr-rock-dj-profiles/index.html

p. 31: "Fifties rock and roll …" Palmer, "The 50s: A Decade of Music That Changed the World."

CHAPTER 3

p. 40: "Come mothers and fathers ..." Bob Dylan, "The Times They Are a-Changin'" (1964).

p. 41: "It was a sweet surrender ..." Park Putterbaugh, "The British Invasion" *Rolling Stone* (July 14, 1988). https://www.rollingstone.com/music/music-news/the-british-invasion-from-the-beatles-to-the-stones-the-sixties-belonged-to-britain-244870/

p. 43: "It was obvious to me ..." Bob Dylan, quoted in Andrew Grant Jackson, 1965: *The Most Revolutionary Year in Music* (New York: Thomas Dunne Books, 2015), p. 10

p. 43: "Combined, the Beatles and Dylan ..." Mikal Gilmore, "Bob Dylan, the Beatles, and the Rock of the Sixties," *Rolling Stone* (August 23, 1990). https://www.rollingstone.com/music/music-news/bob-dylan-the-beatles-and-the-rock-of-the-sixties-176221/

P. 44: "I would come to the South ..." Smokey Robinson, quoted in Ron Thibodeaux, "My Smokey Valentine," (New Orleans) *Times-Picayune*, February 14, 2009.

CHAPTER 5

p. 77: "We all love music ..." Dave Grohl, quoted in Alan di Perna, "Absolutely Foobulous," *Guitar World* (August 1997). http://www.fooarchive.com/features/guitarworld.htm

p. 78: "It's difficult to describe to people ..." John Perry Barlow, "Napster's Enormous Music Room," *New York Times* (August 6, 2000). www.nytimes.com/library/review/080600napster-review.html

p. 80: "Mongolians are not just taking ..." Thalea Stokes, quoted in Katya Cengel, "How a Mongolian Heavy Metal Band Got Millions of YouTube Views," National Public Radio (January 5, 2019). https://www.npr.org/sections/goatsandsoda/2019/01/05/680528912/how-a-mongolian-heavy-metal-band-got-millions-of-youtube-views

p. 82: "Rock 'n' roll certainly is ..." Bill Flanagan, "Is Rock 'n' Roll Dead, or Just Old?" *New York Times* (November 19, 2016). https://www.nytimes.com/2016/11/20/opinion/.../is-rock-n-roll-dead-or-just-old.html

1929: Les Paul creates the first crude electric guitar.

1951: The Gibson Guitar Company begins work on the first solid-body electric guitar. Cleveland DJ Alan Freed launches *The Moon Dog Rock 'n' Roll House Party* on radio station WJW. In March, Jackie Brenston and His Delta Cats release "Rocket 88," which some people regard as the first rock and roll song.

1954: Bill Haley and the Comets record "Rock around the Clock," which becomes the first big rock hit the next year.

1956: On September 9, Elvis Presley performs on the *Ed Sullivan Show*.

1959: Rock stars Buddy Holly, Richie Valens, and JP "Big Bopper" Richardson die in a plane crash.

1960: Motown Records is established.

1964: In January, Bob Dylan's song "The Times They Are a-Changin'" is released. It becomes an anthem of the younger generation. On February 9, the Beatles are introduced to America on the *Ed Sullivan Show*, starting the British Invasion.

1967: In June, the Beatles release *Sgt. Pepper's Lonely Heart's Club Band*, considered by many critics to be the best rock album of all time.

1969: In August, a three-day music festival at Woodstock draws more than 400,000 fans, and features some of the biggest rock acts.

1971: George Harrison produces the Concert for Bangladesh, which raises money for that South Asian country.

1977: Elvis Presley dies at his home in Memphis, Tennessee.

1981: MTV begins broadcasting on cable TV on August 1.

1985: Live Aid raises $70 million for African famine relief by holding rock concerts in London and Philadelphia.

1991: Nirvana's second album, *Nevermind*, becomes a major hit and launches the popularity of grunge.

2001: Many rock stars perform a benefit concert for the victims of the September 11 terrorist attacks.

2012: The Foo Fighters win five Grammy Awards, including the award for Best Rock Album, for Wasting Light.

2018: Sister Rosetta Tharpe is inducted into the Rock and Roll Hall of Fame as an "early influence" on the musical genre.

Buck, Kevin. *A Concise History of Rock 'n' Roll*. Glen Rock, PA: Year of the Book, 2018.

Dakers, Diane. *The Beatles: Leading the British Invasion*. New York: Crabtree Publishing, 2013.

Farseth, Erik. *American Rock: Guitar Heroes, Punks, and Metalheads*. New York: 21st Century Books, 2012

Kallen, Stuart A. *The History of Rock and Roll*. Farmington Hills, Mich.: Lucent Books, 2012.

Larson, Thomas. *History of Rock and Roll*, 5th ed. New York: Rhapsody Publishing, 2019 McDougall, Chros. *Kurt Cobain: Alternative Rock Innovator*. North Mankato, Minn.: Abdo, 2012.

O'Connor, Jim. *Who Is Bob Dylan?* New York: Grosset and Dunlap, 2013.

Wallenfeldt, Jeff. *The Birth of Rock & Roll: Music in the 1950s through the 1960s*. New York: Rosen, 2012.

INTERNET RESOURCES

http://www.rollingstone.com
The award-winning magazine Rolling Stone has been covering rock and popular music since the 1960s. Under the "music features" tab at the site are links to long article on rock music in each decade, as well as articles on the most influential rock musicians.

http://www.rockhall.com/
The website of the Rock and Roll Hall of Fame includes biographies of performers that have been inducted into the hall, articles on Rock music history, photos and videos, news about upcoming shows and events, and other information.

http://www.thebeatles.com
The official website of The Beatles has information about the band and its recordings, song lyrics, photos and video clips, and links to snippets of their music.

https://www.elvis.com
The online home of the King of Rock 'n' Roll features biographical information about Elvis and his beloved Graceland Mansion in Memphis,Tennessee.

http://www.bobdylan.com
The official Bob Dylan website features news about the rock legend, information about his songs and albums, tour dates, and more.

http://www.rollingstones.com
The Rolling Stones official website has information about this legendary group that has been called the "world's greatest rock and roll band."

http://www.rockandrollforever.org
The Rock and Roll Forever Foundation has developed a national curriculum initiative for middle school and high school students, which includes lesson plans for social studies, general music, language arts, media studies, and other classes.

INDEX

INDEX

Napster, 78–79
Nelson, Ricky, 26
New Wave music, 67–68
Nirvana, 75, 77

Palmer, Robert, 18, 21, 33
Parks, Rosa, 22
Paul, Les, 10
payola, 30–31, 33
Pearl Jam, 76–77
Penniman, Richard Wayne. See Little
    Richard
Phillips, Sam, 15–16, 17, 24
Pink Floyd, 64
power ballads, 59–60
Presley, Elvis, 6, 24, 26, 32, 33, 81
progressive rock music, 63–64
punk rock, 63, 64–65

Queen, 56–58, 62

radio and radio stations
    AM vs. FM, 49–50
    influence of, 11, 30, 80
record albums. See album formats
REM, 74
rhythm and blues music, 9, 14–15
Richards, Keith, 37, 41–43
Richardson, JP "Big Bopper," 34
Robinson, Smokey, 44
rock and roll
    in the 1950s, 21–34
    in the 1960s, 37–50
    future of, 82
    impact on society, 10–11, 22, 33, 40–41,
        43–44, 46, 49–50, 68–70
    origins of, 7–18
    vs. rock music, 49–50
    See also albums; rock music; songs
Rock and Roll Hall of Fame and Museum, 17
rock music
    future of, 82
    impact on society, 63, 64–65, 68–70

vs. rock and roll, 49–50
sub-genres of, 53–68
    See also albums; rock and roll; songs
Rolling Stones, 41–43

segregation, 8–10, 22
Sex Pistols, 64
soft rock, 53–55
songs
    "Ain't that a Shame," 29
    "Alive," 76
    "Anarchy in the UK," 64
    "Another One Bites the Dust," 58
    "Barbeque Bust," 18
    "Bennie and the Jets," 62
    "Beth," 59–60
    "Birdhouse in Your Soul," 74
    "Blowing in the Wind," 40
    "Blueberry Hill," 29
    "Blue Suede Shoes," 26
    "Bohemian Rhapsody," 56
    "Candle in the Wind," 62
    "Charlie Brown," 29
    "Come As You Are," 75
    "Crazy Little Thing Called Love," 58
    "Crocodile Rock," 62
    "Dangerous Woman," 18
    "Daughter," 76
    "Detroit Rock City," 59
    "Don't Be Cruel," 6, 26
    "Do They Know It's Christmas?," 69
    "Dream On," 60
    "Everyday," 28
    "Faithfully," 60
    "Get Off of My Cloud," 43
    "God Save the Queen," 64
    "Good Golly Miss Molly," 29
    "Good Rocking Tonight," 16
    "Hard Rain's a-Gonna Fall," 40
    "Heartbreak Hotel," 6, 26
    "Honky Tonk Women," 42
    "Hound Dog," 6, 26
    "I Can't Get No Satisfaction," 42

AUTHOR'S BIOGRAPHY

JAMES JORDAN is a freelance writer who lives in rural Kansas. He has thirty years of experience in the newspaper business and is semi-retired. He was a teenager in the 1980s, which some regard as the heyday of rock and roll. James has won state press association awards for writing, photography, and page design in four states. James has been an avid music fan as long as he can remember and has been involved in creating a few music festivals.

CREDITS